Using a traditional spindle, this Navajo woman practices the centuries-old skills necessary to create spun wool for rug weaving. The Navajo people are world famous for their skill as weavers.

A plains Indian warrior, in a feathered war bonnet, beats a tattoo. The throbbing of drums is much a part of the plains Indians life.

"Happy Faces". Two smiling Indian children, from Monument Valley in Arizona, seem to have stepped out of America's ancient past.

Sioux Indians, seen here outfitted in traditi dress for a powwow, are plains Indians, mas of hunting and the ho

Members of the Apache Mountain Spirit Dancers perform "coming out" rites for these two young girls.

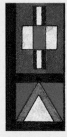

A Kachina dancer of the Hopi tribe.

Members of the Arapaho tribe from the plains of Oklahoma are dressed in traditional finery for a powwow in Flagstaff, Arizona.

This Apache girl proudly displays her traditional dress.

Dressed in buckskin, beading and brightly colored feathers,
Indians prepare for one of the many powwows held annually.

Evangeline Talahaftewa, talented Indian basket
weaver, practices her ancient art.

Two lovely Zuni
girls in
traditional
finery.

Indians have had the use of horses since the arrival of the
Spanish. They play an important part in Indian life today.

National Park Service

CANYON DE CHELLY NATIONAL MONUMENT - ARIZONA

Sheltered beneath sheer sandstone rock faces for over 1,000 years, the Anasazi Indians built multi-roomed cities such as this one known as the "White House" for its light colored mud facing. Here, protected by the cliffs, they established a community lifestyle. The women gardened on the plateaus or the canyon floor and the men hunted the abundant game.

The chore of carrying water up the precarious ladders and handholds carved in the rock face must have been a never ending one. Fragments of beautifully crafted pottery containers used to transport and store water have been found here.

Canyon de Chelly may be reached on paved roads from Gallup, New Mexico via Window Rock; from Holbrook, or Keams Canyon through the Navajo and Hopi Reservations.

CASA GRANDE RUINS NATIONAL MONUMENT ARIZONA

Rising like a castle on a vast plain near the Gila River south of present-day Phoenix, Casa Grande was the home of the Hohokam Indians. Built in the 12th century, the three-story structure stood at the center of a walled caliche, or town. The caliches became hubs for scattered surrounding villages.

The monument grounds, about a mile north of Coolidge on Highway 87, contain about 60 prehistoric sites and are open 7 a.m. to 6 p.m. daily.

Monuments

MONTEZUMA CASTLE NATIONAL MONUMENT ARIZONA

Midway between Flagstaff and Phoenix near Camp Verde on I-17 sits this 20-room structure built in the 12th century by Sinagua Indians. Tucked into a virtually impregnable natural cavern 100 feet above the valley floor with fertile lands below and on nearby terraces and a reliable water supply from the valley creek, this provided a perfect location for these agricultural Indians.

This young Indian mother, Pricilla Nuvamza, wearing prehistoric shell necklaces, seems to have stepped out of the distant past, her daughter safely carried in a hand woven cradleboard much like those used by her ancestors.

MONTEZUMA WELL NATIONAL MONUMENT ARIZONA

North on I-17 a few miles from Montezuma Castle is the McGuireville turnoff where a side road leads you to this natural well. Created by the collapse of a huge underground cavern, this limestone sink is fed by continuously flowing springs as it was in ancient times. Traces of irrigation ditches built by Hohokam and Sinagua Indians may still be seen.

Cliff dwellings and a Hohokam pithouse, the forerunner of their later above ground dwellings, may also be toured.

NAVAJO NATIONAL MONUMENT - ARIZONA

Around A.D. 1250, the Kayenta, an Anasazi people, began building cliff dwellings. The best known are Betatakin, Inscription House and Keet Seel (pictured above). All have been preserved at Navajo National Monument two miles northeast of Tuba City on U.S 160 or 20 miles southwest of Kayenta.

Constructed of mud mortared masonry painstakingly built into cliff shelves 40 feet and more above the valley floor, the Kayenta built a city that could be defended by nothing more than a handful of children. Several of the locations may also have been served by running streams, making them virtually self-

contained fortresses.

Visitors may still see the living quarters, storage rooms, kivas and streets looking much like they must have in 1300 when the Kayenta Anasazi abandoned them, probably due to a severe and protracted drought.

TONTO NATIONAL MONUMENT ARIZONA

Sheltered in the shadow of a massive sandstone shelf the Salado ("salty") Indians built complex houses a thousand feet above the Salt River Valley about A.D. 900. In the river valley they cultivated corn, beans, squash, amaranth and cotton. Wild plants including yucca, mesquite and saguaro cactus provided food and fabric dyes. Pottery specimens have been found molded to resemble the human form.

Open 8 a.m. to 5 p.m. daily, Tonto National Monument may be reached from Phoenix via U.S. 60-70 to Apache Junction, then left on Az-88 along the scenic Apache Trail to Roosevelt. Those arriving from the east may take U.S. 60-70 to Globe and Az-88. The visitors center is located three miles from Roosevelt.

TUZIGOOT NATIONAL MONUMENT - ARIZONA

Sitting like a crown on the summit of a 120 foot ridge above the Verde Valley are the remains of Sinaguan village built around 1125. The Sinaguan Indians (from the Spanish words for without water) were dry land farmers who eked out their crops on the inhospitable desert landscape of central Arizona.

This life-sized diorama in the Tuzigoot National Monument Museum has been constructed to show an example of what the interior of a Sinagua Indian home in the Verde Valley looked like in the 12th century.

Located in Midstate, take I-17 to the Clarkdale-Cottonwood exit.

TUMACACORI NATIONAL MONUMENT ARIZONA

The Spanish influence upon the Indians of what is now Arizona began to be felt in the late 1600's when missionary priests arrived from Mexico to convert the Indians from their religious beliefs to Christianity.

Father Eusebio Kino, a Spanish priest, visited the small Pima Indian village of Tumacacori in 1691 and established his mission. The name comes from a Pima Indian word, "tsu-ma-ka-kori", meaning "curved peak." Construction of the present church was begun in about 1800 by Franciscan Fathers.

Tumacacori is 48 miles south of Tucson or 89 miles north of Nogales and accessible by paved roads year round.

WUPATKI NATIONAL MONUMENT - ARIZONA

North of Flagstaff in an area of approximately one square mile lie more than 100 sites and 2,000 Indian ruins of the ancient Anasazi, "The Ancient Ones". The ruins here include small earth lodges, kivas and large pueblos. An intermixing of Indian cultures including Cohonino and Sinagua took place at Wupatki. There is also evidence to indicate Hohokam and Mogollon influences.

Wupatki National Monument is North of Flagstaff of U.S. 89 and then east 14 miles on a well paved road 14 miles to the visitor center.

WALNUT CANYON NATIONAL MONUMENT ARIZONA

Walnut Canyon provided a safe haven for the Sinagua Indians when they settled here in the 12th century and built more than 300 small cliff rooms terraced up the side of the verdant canyon. Fertile land, abundant water and forests made this an ideal location. The Sinagua were free to farm the soil and practice and refine their arts in weaving and pottery.

AZTEC RUINS NATIONAL MONUMENT NEW MEXICO

One of the most well preserved ruins of the ancient Anasazi culture is Aztec Ruins. The stone walls, mortared with adobe, have withstood over 800 years of weathering. The original builders of the pueblo abandoned it for reasons unknown around A.D. 1130. The pueblo was reoccupied by another culture of people in the 1200s.

CHACO CULTURE NATIONAL HISTORICAL PARK
NEW MEXICO

During the 11th and 12th centuries the Anasazi Indians lifestyle of pueblo building and farming flourished in what scholars call the Chaco Phenomenon in northwestern New Mexico. Here amidst isolated mesas, dusty washes and eroding winds the Chacoans erected multistoried towns. It is estimated that several thousand people resided here. Pueblo Bonito, the largest of them, had more than 650 rooms.

When arriving from the north, take N.M. 44 and turn off at Blanco Trading Post. Follow N.M. 57 for 23 miles to the north entrance. From the south, take N.M. 57 north from I-40 at Thoreau for 44 miles. A marked turn-off gives access to a 20-mile unpaved road and the south entrance. No services are available at the park.

BANDELIER NATIONAL MONUMENT
NEW MEXICO

Bandelier National Monument, 46 miles west of Santa Fe, was named for Swiss-born Adolph Bandelier who rode a mule thousands of miles in search of prehistoric sites in the Southwest. He lived among the descendants of these tribes, following their leads, and discovered a number of ancient settlements, among them the ruins of Frijoles Canyon, which now carries his name.

It is thought these ruins were occupied before the Spanish advances into the Southwest. Pottery shards and cotton cloth found at the site indicate that the Indians here were farmers and probably had looms for weaving.

The pueblos of Tyuonyi and Tsankawi appear to have been occupied until around 1550 when they too were abandoned. To reach Bandelier National Monument take U.S. 285 north to Pojoaque, turn west on State Route 4. You may also travel through the scenic Jemez country from Albuquerque, weather permitting.

EL MORRO NATIONAL MONUMENT - NEW MEXICO

Named for the Spanish conquistadors of the 17th century, El Morro claims a history much older than this. Perched atop the 200 foot sandstone mesa have been found ruins of Zuni Indian pueblos abandoned long before the coming of the Spanish. Here also can be found some of America's earliest graffiti. Hundreds of petroglyphs, ancient inscription, carved into the face of the rock, allow modern mankind to read and attempt to decipher the messages left by this prehistoric people.

El Morro is located 43 miles west of Grants via N.M. 53 or 58 miles southwest of Gallup via N.M. 32 and 53. There are campground and picnic areas at the monument.

GILA CLIFF DWELLINGS NATIONAL MONUMENT NEW MEXICO

Lying 44 miles north of Silver City at the edge of the Gila Wilderness Area, Gila Cliff Dwellings National Monument is significant because the earliest ruins in the area are those of the pit houses of the Mongollon people who lived here about 500 A.D. May be reached via a 44-mile drive north of Silver City on State Highway 15. Visiting hours depend on the season.

HOVENWEEP NATIONAL MONUMENT
UTAH/COLORADO

In the high mesa country of southwestern Colorado and southeastern Utah, referred to as the Four Corners area, can be found the ruins of other Anasazi Indians. Early settlers built pit houses which later gave way to two-and three-storied structures constructed of native stone and mortared with adobe mud.

It is suggested that the towers may have served as astronomical observatories, allowing the priests of the tribe to forecast weather and moon cycles for planting and ceremonies. Others believe the towers served strictly religious purposes or were used as lookout towers to spot approaching enemies.

PECOS NATIONAL MONUMENT
NEW MEXICO

These multi-storied pueblos built of native stone mortared with mud built around a central plaza on a rocky ridge were home to the Pecos Indians from about 1450 until well into the 17th century. A knowledge of irrigation allowed these people to produce healthy crops of corn and squash.

Although farming was the Pecos' chief occupation, they also developed a thriving enterprise in trade, being located between the nomadic buffalo hunters of the plains and the Indians of the Rio Grande.

MESA VERDE NATIONAL PARK - COLORADO

The largest archaeological preserve in the United States is located at Mesa Verde near Cortes in the southwest corner of present day Colorado. Here, on a majestic plateau rising abruptly out of semi-arid land. The Anasazi built some of their finest architecture. And here they made their homes for more than 700 years, until the end of the 13th century A.D. Some of the most extraordinary finds in the Southwest have been made within this 20-mile long stretch. Cliff Palace, Mesa Verde's largest pueblo, had 200 rooms and 23 kivas or ceremonial chambers. Other pueblos within Mesa Verde were nearly as large as Cliff Palace. In its peak Mesa Verde is thought to have been home to as many as 7,000 men, women and children.

SAGUARO NATIONAL MONUMENT - ARIZONA

Messages from ancient times, petroglyphs have been found throughout the Southwest. Like these on Signal Hill at the Tucson Mountain Unit of the Saguaro National Monument, they offer modern investigators a glimpse into the prehistoric lives of the "Ancient Ones", the Anasazi People who are the ancestors of many of today's Indian tribes.

NAVAJO

"The People" as the Navajo call themselves, live today on the largest Indian reservation in the United States comprised mainly of land in northeastern Arizona, southeastern Utah, and northwestern New Mexico.

Originally fierce nomadic hunters, the ancestors of the Navajo moved into the southwest about 1500. Along with their relatives, the Apache, they established dominance over the regions sedentary Pueblo builders.

The Navajo learned from their neighbors the skilled trades of weaving blankets, basket weaving, pottery making, the carving of turquoise ornaments, beads, and tools. Preferring the semi-nomadic life they never adopted the building of Pueblos preferring to live in hogans of timber and poles covered with bark and mud. Spanish soldiers and settlers brought horses and sheep. Today raising sheep is a primary industry.

Well known for their skill in working silver and turquoise, the Navajo men learned their craft from the Mexicans in the early 1800's. Using designs adapted from many sources, craftsmen created beautifully detailed pieces which they set with native turquoise.

Pictured above is a collection of fine Indian jewelry.

Joseph Lonewolf is noted for his carved pottery.

A Navajo woman shows her handcrafted pottery jar.

This proud Navajo mother carries her child in a cradleboard much like those used by her ancestors.

Navajo Indians on horseback travel across Monument Valley whose spires, buttes and monuments tower over the mile-high valley by a thousand feet or more. The landscape speaks eloquently of nature's works with wind, rain and time.

Navajo men dressed in
ceremonial finery.

Monument Valley inspires this
Navajo weaver

Navajo Indian arts have been
passed down from generation to
generation, many remaining
unchanged from ancient times.
Potters still form their pots using
the coil method, adding colored
slips (liquid clays) to create
striking designs. Firings are still
done the traditional way.
Navajo weaving is known and
collected throughout the world.
Each is hand-woven from wool
grown, carded, dyed and spun
on the reservation. Patterns vary
from weaver to weaver and
include ancient designs and
modern adaptations.

Much of the Navajo lifestyle is unchanged. Many women still wear the traditional velveteen tops decorated with silver, and long full skirts of velveteen or calico.

Some still live in hogans although most now have stoves for heat and cooking. Foods also have changed little. Meals of mutton and squash or corn are often served (a favorite of The People.) The woman at left is shown making fried bread over an open fire.

Sand-paintings have been used for centuries to aid in healing.

Navajo pitch-covered water jars woven by ancient methods.

A Navajo woman works on a beautifully detailed blanket.

HOPI

Walpi, 600 feet above the desert, home to the Hopi Indians for 1,000 years.

Rich in color and design, Hopi baskets are prized artifacts.

The Hopita from which the name Hopi derives, means "gentle people". Their ancestry can be traced back to the ancient Mogollon tribes who dwelled here 2000 years ago.

Many Hopis still cling to the quaint world of yesterday practicing ancient customs and rituals.

The Hopis built two-storied pueblos of mud-mortared stone. The original buildings had no doors or windows and were entered through a hole in the roof.

Each household grew its own crops of corn, beans and squash. Tending the crops was the men's work. They also hunted wild game and it was their responsibility to weave cloth for the entire family. Basketry, pottery and general household routine was woman's work. The women also ground the grain for pika, the paper-thin bread that was the Hopis' staple.

Kachinas are supernatural beings with vast powers and are worshipped by the Hopis.

Distinctive pottery of the Hopis.

The Hopis, like all Indians of the great Southwest, are the product of ancestry and environment. The Hopi are not great warriors or renowned hunters. They are extraordinary potters and weavers, talented craftspeople, people who live in harmony with the land, using its resources to produce crops, intricate basketry and beautiful pottery.

Their religion stems from ancient times. The Kachinas, or spirits, dominate their religious rituals. Hopi children learn of the Kachinas early in life. Among their most treasured possessions are wooden kachina dolls. Replicas of the Kachinas are carved from cottonwood root and are very popular with collectors.

A Hopi basket hangs on the wall behind an ancient corn meal grinding stone and metate.

A Hopi plaiting technique is demonstrated here in this unfinished plaque.

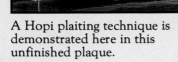

morning kachina oll carved by Tino ouvella. The Hopi illage of Walpi is silouetted in the ackground.

Hopi basketry shows intricate workmanship.

PAPAGO

The Mission San Xavier on the Papago Reservation near Tucson.

A Papago woman makes a basket in the time-honored way.

The fruit of the giant saguaro cactus is prized by the Papago.

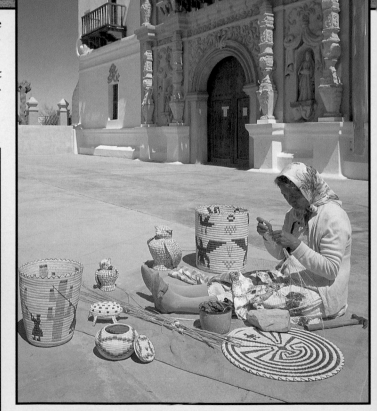

Southern Arizona is home to the Papago Indians, direct descendants of the ancient Hohokum tribe. The Papagos were originally a seminomadic tribe, traveling to summer "field villages" in the desert where heavy rains provided water for their crops of pumpkins, beans and corn. Winters found them returning to their "well villages" near streams and springs in the mountains. Here they depended mostly upon hunting for food.

The arrival of Spanish missionaries dramatically changed the lifestyle of the Papago Indians. They helped build missions such as San Xavier and wove the missionaries beliefs into their own religious rituals.

Today the Papago, a people of gentle nature, enjoy an economy composed of cattle, agriculture and copper mining. All the reservations share one common product, however. The Papago produce more baskets than any other tribe in the United States. Their workmanship and quality is second to none.

The Papago Indians combine their religious culture with that of the Catholic mission.

An unusual basket doll example of Papago artistry.

The intricate work is apparent in this split-stitch basket and lid.

Beautiful examples of Apache basketry on San Carlos Reservation.

An Apache woman making a burden basket.

Apache maidens dressed in traditional costumes, decorated with beadwork and fringe.

A finished burden basket dating from the early 1900's.

The Apaches were late arrivals in the Southwest. They came originally from Canada about 500 years ago. For centuries, they were known as ferocious warriors and raiders. Mexican and U.S settlers came to dread Apache warriors but few were as feared as Geronimo. A man of peace for nearly 10 years, Geronimo was transformed into a man of vengeance when Mexican troops killed his family in 1859. In 1886 he finally surrendered to U.S. troops.

The Apache tribes of today are located in several areas: the Mescalero in south-central New Mexico, the Jicarillo in northeastern New Mexico, the Chiricahua in New Mexico and southern Arizona, and the Western Apache in northern and southern Tonto, Cibecue, White Mountain and San Carlos.

The Apache people honor many ancient traditions.

The lifestyle of the once ferocious Apache people today revolves around the land. Cattle and timber are their main income producers. The Apache have come to treasure their unspoiled lands and nourish their ancient culture as can be seen in their basket weaving and treasured rituals.

HAVASUPAI

Within the depths of the Grand Canyon lies the reservation of the Havasupai Indians whose name means "Blue Water People". The village of Supai has been home to the Havasupai for more than 900 years.

Surrounded by sheer cliffs 2000 to 4000 feet high, the Havasupai live in a paradise of verdant lands. Three waterfalls provide a spectacular backdrop for this quiet people and the sparkling blue waters of Havasu Creek lends its name to the tribe.

The trails discovered by Father Garces in 1776 are still the only ground routes into the canyon of the Havasupai.

The Havasupai still practice their ancient crafts and religion. The invention of the modern helicopter has made travel into the canyon easier in recent years but much of their supplies, including the U.S. mail, still enters the canyon by horse- or mule-back.

Havasu Falls as viewed from the trail leading to the reservation.

The Havasupai village seems to blend perfectly with the surrounding canyon.

SANTA CLARA

SAN ILDEFONSO

Some of the most beautiful pottery in the world comes from the Santa Clara and San Ildefonso Pueblos located north of Santa Fe, New Mexico. Many pieces are elaborately decorated with ancient figures. Shown here are three pottery wedding vases.

The Santa Clara and San Ildefonso Pueblos are also noted for their fine blackware pottery.

The pottery of Santa Clara and San Ildefonso, built and fired in the ancient way, is much sought after and highly prized by collectors the world over.

TAOS PUEBLO

The homes of Taos Pueblo.

Taos Pueblo's first residents may have been fleeing the drought in Mesa Verde over 700 years ago. Here they found a mountain stream and beautiful lake. In this place that must have looked like Heaven to the water starved people, they built their homes following the ancient styles of stone and adobe. The entrances were reachable only by ladder, which could be quickly pulled up in case of attack. Today, Taos is divided by its mountain stream into North Pueblo and South Pueblo.

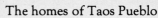

A warrior performs a tribal dance accompanied by the beating of a drum.

 # ACOMA

Acoma, The City of the Sky, sits nearly 400 feet above the New Mexico plain on its rocky fortress. It is the oldest continuously occupied home of America's first residents. The ancient Acomas descended tortuous toehold trails to tend their fields below. The Acoma Indians of today still farm those same fields.

Noted as fine weavers and basketmakers, the Acomas are perhaps best known for their striking pottery.

A display of traditional Acoma whiteware pottery.

At Zuni Pueblo, due south of Gallup, New Mexico, the potter still leaves a break in the line drawn around a jar's neck as her ancestors have since ancient times. She believes her life would end if she closed the "road". The Zuni pottery of today is little changed from that produced by the Indian's ancestors The Zuni are also noted for their silversmithing and have become famous for the fine jewelry they produce. The Zuni's ancestors wore turquoise beads and earrings and encrusted cradles and doorways with the magical blue stones to ward off evil.

Zuni women balancing ollas (water jars) on their heads.

Zuni maids display traditional outfits. Each shows her dramatic turquoise jewelry.